FARM ANIMALS

CHICKENS

by Kathryn Clay

raintree
a Capstone company — publishers for children

Raintree is an imprint of Capstone Global Library Limited, a company incorporated in England and Wales having its registered office at 264 Banbury Road, Oxford, OX2 7DY – Registered company number: 6695582

www.raintree.co.uk
myorders@raintree.co.uk

Edited by Erika L. Shores
Designed by Ashlee Suker
Picture research by Marcie Spence
Production by Eric Manske

ISBN 978 1 4747 1901 8
20 19 18 17 16 15
10 9 8 7 6 5 4 3 2 1

British Library Cataloguing in Publication Data
A full catalogue record for this book is available from the British Library.

Photo Credits
Alamy Images: D. Hurst, 17, Greg Wright, 21; iStockphoto: Lawrence Sawyer, 19; Shutterstock: Borko Ciric, 13, Groomee, 11, krugloff, 15, liubomir, 7, Lurii Konoval, cover, 1, tepic, 5, Tomas Sereda, 9

We would like to thank Gail Saunders-Smith, PhD, and Dr. Celina Johnson for their invaluable help in the preparation of this book.

Note to Parents and Teachers

This book describes and illustrates chickens. The images support early readers in understanding the text. The repetition of words and phrases helps early readers learn new words. This book also introduces early readers to subject-specific vocabulary, which is defined in the Glossary section. Early readers may need assistance to read some words and to use the Table of contents, Glossary, Read more, Internet sites and Index sections of the book.

Printed and bound in China.

Contents

Meet the chickens

Cock-a-doodle-doo!

An adult male chicken crows as

the sun rises.

Chickens dash around the farm.

Most chickens have white,

brown, black or red feathers.

They peck with sharp beaks.

Below the beak of some chickens

is a red flap of skin called a wattle.

wattle

Chickens weigh about

3 kilogrammes (7 pounds).

Chickens can only fly short distances.

Their small wings cannot lift their

heavy bodies.

New life

Male chickens are called cocks.

Hens are female chickens.

Only hens lay eggs.

cock

hen

Hens sit on eggs to keep them warm.

Crack! Eggs hatch after 21 days.

Young chickens are called chicks.

On the farm

Chickens eat feed made
of corn, wheat and seeds.
Chickens also scratch the ground
for insects and worms.

Farmers raise chickens for eggs and meat. Farmers collect eggs twice a day. Eggs are white, brown, tawny, blue or green. Supermarkets sell white or brown eggs.

Chickens are also kept as pets.

Some chickens let you hold them.

They may eat out of your hand.

Foxes try to attack chickens at night.

Chickens stay safe in coops

made of wire and wood.

Glossary

beak hard front part of the mouths of birds

cock adult male chicken

coop small building where chickens stay safe and lay eggs

dash move quickly and suddenly

hatch break out of a shell

hen female chicken

peck pick at something

wattle piece of skin that hangs down from the chin of some birds

Read more

Farm Animals (Say & Point Picture Book), Nicola Tuxworth (Armadillo Books, 2015)

Farm Animals (World of Farming), Nancy Dickmann (Heinemann Library, 2011)

Henrietta's Guide to Caring for Your Chickens (Pets' Guides), Isabel Thomas (Heinemann Library, 2015)

Websites

discoverykids.com/category/animals/
Learn facts about animals and check out photos of all sorts of animals on this website.

kids.nationalgeographic.com/animals
Search for different sorts of animals and learn where they live, what they eat and more.

Index